BASEMENT STORE

HANDBOOKS OF EUROPEAN NATIONAL DANCES

EDITED BY
VIOLET ALFORD

DANCES OF SWEDEN

Plate I
Uppland

DANCES of SWEDEN

ERIK SALVÉN

PUBLISHED

UNDER THE AUSPICES OF

THE ROYAL ACADEMY OF DANCING

AND THE

LING PHYSICAL EDUCATION ASSOCIATION

LONDON

MAX PARRISH & COMPANY

FIRST PUBLISHED IN 1949 BY
MAX PARRISH & CO LIMITED
51A RATHBONE PLACE LONDON W.1
IN ASSOCIATION WITH
ADPRINT LIMITED LONDON

TRANSLATED BY
VERONICA WRIGHT
ILLUSTRATED BY
E. JOYCE STONE
ASSISTANT EDITOR
YVONNE MOYSE

PRINTED IN GREAT BRITAIN
BY JARROLD AND SONS LTD NORWICH
ON MELLOTEX BOOK PAPER MADE BY
TULLIS RUSSELL AND CO LTD MARKINCH SCOTLAND
MUSIC PHOTO-SET BY
WOLFGANG PHILIPP ZURICH-HINTEREGG

CONTENTS

Illustrations in Colour, pages 2, 19, 30, 31
Map of Sweden, page 6

Most dances have their origins in folk dances and have developed into the social dances used by the townsfolk and gentry. Foreign dances have come into fashion also and these, with the social dances, have gone back to the people and again become folk dances. This give-and-take movement goes on perpetually and must always be taken into account.*

We find no reliable authority for the presence of the dance in Sweden until written history begins. In the medieval *Erik's Chronicle* we read that when King Valdemar, son of Birger Jarl, founder of Stockholm, celebrated his wedding in the thirteenth century, dances were part of the festivities.

It is typical that the first mention of dancing in Swedish literature should be in connection with a wedding. The greatest occasion in a man's life was his wedding. Celebrations went on for several days, and most of our dances and other customs would have perished but for their inclusion in marriage feasts. To-day the big country wedding is probably the only remaining occasion on which our ancient dances are used by the peasants to whom they belong.

* This sketch follows to a great extent Mats Rehnberg's *Swedish Folk Dances* (Picture books of the Nordiska Museum and Skansen, No. 9. Stockholm, 1939).

Medieval folk songs frequently mention the dance, for they were largely sung as dance-songs. The dancers would form a long chain, holding hands. At their head went the leader, setting the time and singing the song's many verses, all the dancers joining in the chorus after each verse. Wave upon wave of new dances have swept over the country in the centuries succeeding the Middle Ages, changing or crowding out the earlier ones. In spite however of fashion, the 'long dance' has lived on up to our day; there can scarcely be anyone in our country who has not at one time or another taken part in a long dance. Sometimes these chains are started to keep life in one's body when the Spring fires and the barrels of pitch are lit on a bitter Easter Eve, or on Walpurgis Night (April 30); sometimes round the swaying Midsummer maypole. In many parts of the country, no Christmas feast or wedding is considered correct that does not finish with all the guests—grandmothers not excepted—winding their way through all the rooms in a boisterous chain, and, in rustic surroundings, out among the sheds and outhouses too. In certain districts, dancers continue in the long dance for hours, from farm to farm, from cottage to cottage.

When the long dance was held round the Spring fire or the maypole, round the bridal couple or the musician, the chain often joined into a ring. When the Christmas tree reached our country from Germany at the end of the eighteenth century, it became a lively centre for the ring dance. Thus can importation impart life to an old dance form. That the celebration of Christmas helped in the preservation of this dance is clear by its frequently being called *Juldans* (Yule dance) from that time.

The ring was particularly suitable for dramatic action. The occasionally dramatic contents of medieval folk songs suggest a little play during the dance. As a rule this consisted of the old theme, a young man seeking a girl, or vice versa, so as to form a pair. This done, the two dance with one another, sometimes alone in the ring, sometimes followed by all the pairs. The introduction of rollicking dancing in pairs at the end of the Middle Ages was no novelty to Sweden, but merely a prolongation of the finale in the older dances. But long dance and ring dance came to form an often-recurring element in the various folk dances of later years, with the ever-growing intricacy of their figures.

At the great festivals of bygone times, everyone not incapacitated by sickness or infirmity took part in the dancing. In districts specially given to dance—Bergslagen in central Sweden for one—we have found the Gubbdunder (literally, gaffer-thunderings), when old people danced, keeping young ones out. But usually it was the youth of our country who gathered of old for dancing at appointed spots, of which place-names bear witness. During the warm season it might be in the village street, at a well, or on an open space or bridge. In winter, they collected indoors in cottages or homesteads. Old furniture, which was fixed to the wall, left plenty of room in the middle of the floor. Everyone taking part had to contribute something to the food and drink, and perhaps a little gift to the musician, who usually played the fiddle or the flute, but from the latter half of the nineteenth century the concertina.

In the fifteenth century special trade or Guild dances are spoken of. Olaus Magnus wrote the often-quoted description of a Sword dance, showing the classic Hilt and Point figure and the culminating lock of swords. He speaks also of a Bow or Arch dance, and of the Hormus dance. His pictures show bands of well-dressed young men who may be Guild members or young men of good families. It is uncertain whether these dances were known among country folk; if so, no traces of them have survived in Sweden.

The most usual cottage folk dance during the last three hundred years has been the Polska. It is derived, as the name shows, from Sweden's intimate relations with Poland round about 1600.* In common with the Renaissance dances at the courts of European princes, the Polska consisted of many figures, usually a slow first part passing into a gyrating second part. It was composed of simple steps and springs, sometimes hopping. The old arrangement, with an alternation between leisurely walking steps and rapid turns, has successfully adapted itself to the most varying circumstances, and almost become the hallmark of the Swedish folk dance, whether it be a simple twirling dance like Hjuling (wheeling) or a whole suite like Huppleken (the hopping game).

A number of variations sprang up with different names. In Värmland, the province of Gösta Berling, and amongst the 'cavaliers', the socially active young men of that province, there was not infrequently a slight knee-bending in the dance, so a curtseying Polska became known as the Värmland Polska. Another is Dalpolska (Dalecarlia Polska), though its most usual designation was probably Slängpolska (Swinging Polska). In certain districts of Dalecarlia whole suites have come into being as at a Renaissance court. The natives of Floda in western Dalecarlia still dance the Hupplek, which got its name from the hopping of the men in the circular march of the first movement to mark the transition to the next figure. The Polska has long been the favourite dance in the greater part of this country, as may be seen by the number of its tunes in country musicians' music books.

In Leksandslåten (the Leksand dance), from the Siljan region, at a certain moment the men try to steal each other's girls—a trick giving rise to amusing and unlooked-for

* See *Dances of Finland* for the Polska.

results. In the round of the second movement, for instance, they sometimes become three or four pairs instead of one. Other Polskas such as Trekarlspolska (Three Fellows' Polska) and Fyramannadans (Four-Man Dance) are characterised by a set of three or four. Akin to the Trekarls-polska is the so-called Ryska Polska (Russian Polska), when an extra man suddenly appears in the dance as a rival and mischief-maker. In Snurrebocken (Twiddle-goat) all the dancers stop at a musical signal to exchange polite compliments and bows; this is assuredly an inspiration from the upper-class French dances, though Snurrebocken is a good example of a folk dance from Hälsingland in Northern Sweden, where the peasants show a certain aristocratic stateliness.

FOREIGN FASHIONS

Polish dances were the fashion at the beginning of the eighteenth century, due to Polish influence among the higher classes. New forms appeared under the name of the old Polska, and the first movement of the old Polska now slipped into 3/4 time. This new dance still bore witness to the land of its birth but, during that century, took on a Frenchified form, Polonaise. Then a dance arose in 3/4 time with improvised figures in a relatively rapid tempo. Its Polish name, Mazurka, comes from the province of Mazovia. While the slow and courtly Polonaise was almost confined to the salons, the livelier Mazurka quickly became a peasant dance during the eighteenth century, and has lived in different forms till the American influence of the twentieth century became too strong for it. Nevertheless if the elderly or middle-aged are asked to vote for a dance, it will generally be the Mazurka.

From France came the Minuet during the eighteenth century. As, however, it was inevitably stylised, the peasants preferred the Polonaise, though it did appear as a ceremonial dance, particularly at big country weddings.

The folk dance, as we said, has often been influenced by society dances and social dances changed to suit the folk. In this way, at the end of the eighteenth century, French Contre-danses yielded the Kadrilj (Quadrille), which has been danced in different forms through the whole of the nineteenth century, principally in south and central Sweden. Numberless versions sprang up in different places, all characterised by the usual four-sided or at any rate rectilinear sets, and a number of courtly elements in the actual execution. In the country, the Quadrille was enriched by the introduction of elements from older native dances, and its formation in its turn influenced other dances.

At the beginning of the nineteenth century a dance in 2/4 time appeared, the Schottische; judging from the form of the name it was probably introduced from Germany. This dance can still be found in different parts of the country, usually with only two figures consisting of several hopping steps forward in open formation, followed by a second movement in closed formation. Earlier, it was frequently elaborated by a whole series of different figures, the pairing-off of different couples, and so on.

Influenced by the 3/4 time of the Polska, a Polka in quick triple time arose in the middle of the nineteenth century. Its name of Hambo (a corruption of Hamburg) indicates its source. The Berlinska, the Hamburgska, the Hamburg Schottisch or Tyska Polka are all off-shoots of the Hambo. After the Waltz, the Hambo is probably the commonest dance still extant from the nineteenth century.

⚜ MODERN FOREIGN INFLUENCES ⚜

In the southern provinces, a style of dancing seems to show that many of the men habitually worked as harvesters in Denmark and Germany. Influences from the lively Norwegian dances are visible in Värmland and West Dalecarlia, recalling the meetings of Swede and Norwegian at markets and on commercial travels. Thus in the Värmland Jössehäradspolska (the Jösse parish Polska), the men turn cartwheels and somersaults, and try to touch the beams across the roof with their feet—a well-known test of agility in Norway. A so-called Norsk Vals (Norwegian Waltz) was danced in Dalecarlia not long ago, and in many villages of the same province we find the Halling, a purely Norwegian dance. The Halling, danced by young men, calls for agility, and consists of gymnastics and rhythmic acrobatics than dancing in the usual sense of the word.

There are quite a number of dances for men in which agility takes first place. In Skarva, or Dans på Skarven (literally Dance on the Join), and also in the similar Dans på Strå (Dance on the Straw), the movements are dictated by the cracks of the floor, by straws or drawn lines, which may not be trodden on during the dance. In the Skåne dance Kopparslagaren (the Coppersmith), and in the Halland Björndans (the Bear dance), certain difficult leg movements have to be executed. There have also been a number of comic dances, usually performed by men only. In the Skåne Skobodans (the Forest-dweller dance), the man swings his leg over his kneeling partner, after which they bow alternately towards and away from each other, all the time bumping into one another. In Gubbdunder (Gaffer-thundering), already mentioned, each man waltzes by himself, at the same time trying to bump his neighbour in the back, and in Örfiladansen (the Ear-boxing dance) they mime accordingly.

THE FOLK-DANCE REVIVAL

Our folk dances were practically swept away in the urbanisation at the end of the nineteenth century, as were most of the characteristics of traditional Swedish peasant culture. But from this decline of folk culture arose the Renaissance movement, preserving a knowledge of the past—in museums. Artur Hazelius began his prodigious work by the creation of the Nordiska Museum and Skansen—the famous open-air museum in Stockholm—models for hundreds of smaller provincial museums. At the Universities the Country Dialect Associations stirred up interest in rural dialect research. In connection with this an interest sprang up in peasant dances, particularly in Uppsala, though it was not until after the institution of Skansen in the 1890's that this interest began to show results. Artur Hazelius took the initiative in the formation of Svenska Folkdansens Vänner (The Friends of the Swedish Folk Dance), his son and successor Gunnar Hazelius in a special Folkvisedanslag (Folk song-dance team). Young people from different districts have been performing the old dances and games at Skansen for nearly sixty years now. Famous peasant musicians from different regions have also been summoned to Skansen.

In the course of this century interest has spread throughout the entire country. Regional costumes, music and dancing take first place in the various movements for preserving local history. These movements are still important and have done much to preserve old buildings and rural peculiarities in the different provinces by means of their societies. Svenska Ungdomsringen för Bygdekultur (Swedish Youth Circle for Local Culture) is the central organisation of the many dance societies. Swedish folk dance has been made known by demonstrations in both Europe and America, and a thorough and scientific research is now devoted to it by music historians and folklorists.

MUSIC

The cowherd's horn and the ancient trumpet seem to be largely responsible for primitive Swedish music such as the tunes for calling the cows, the Vallåtar and Hornlåtar. These are generally in a minor key, the tone-scheme predetermined by the cowherd's simple instrument. Shepherds' and cowmen's songs are often calls to straying animals or signals to each other. These primitive airs grow in richness when other instruments come into play, the violin or some wind instrument. These have given us gånglåtar or march tunes played at weddings and feasts; special names are applied to particular airs such as brudlåt, bridal tune; skänklåt (pouring-out tune) while drinks are poured out, and rolåt, the repose tune, played between the wedding dance and the 'dancing out' of the bride; tiggarlåt, the beggar's tune, played during the collection for the bridal couple; the kryckgånge or crutch tune used for carrying the fiddler to the bride's home riding on the end of the birch tree just felled.

An early collection of folk tunes was made by R. Dybeck in the middle of the last century, whose work is continued by the Swedish Folk Music Commission. *Svenska Låtar*, compiled by Nils Andersson, contains a large collection of dances, tunes and songs from different regions.

Modern Swedish composers have turned to their traditional music for inspiration, and what the folk lyric has been to poetry, folk music has been to music.

COSTUMES

Costumes are not worn everywhere, but where they exist they are jealously guarded by local rules against new fashions creeping in, or styles from other parishes. Newcomers and newly-married people must adopt the costume of their new parish. A wedding dress often belonged to the church, to be lent to brides, who also wore a showy bridal crown of artificial flowers and beads.

Breared parish, Halland, whence comes the Ovraby Quadrille, has a lovely dress made of locally woven stuffs. The man's waistcoat and the girl's bodice are of weaves peculiar to Halland, often found in tapestries of that district. Blue is the predominating colour. Girls wear light-coloured caps, married women dark ones, a knitted band round their stockings just showing over their shoes, and decorative silver buckles on the bodice which serve as hooks and eyes. Young men wear short jackets, their elders a long coat.

The people who dance Renningen, the Weaving dance, wear the dress of Häverö, Uppland. The woman's up-standing cap is the chief characteristic and unique in Sweden. Married women must allow no hair to be seen, so wear a thin stuff decorated with lace over their heads under the cap; girls wear the same high cap but without the cover for the hair. The man wears his holiday costume. The design on his breeches should be noticed and the curve on which his jacket buttons are sewn. Elder men wear long, white homespun coats.

The costume of Floda, Dalecarlia, still worn, is without equal in Sweden for beauty of embroideries. The ver-milion background to the exquisite floral designs is in sharp contrast to the green sleeveless jacket. Boots are now old-fashioned, and shoes would be generally worn for dancing. From this parish comes Huppleken, the Hopping Dance.

OCCASIONS WHEN DANCING MAY BE SEEN

'When the woods and fields are green and flowers are in bloom, and the sun is in the sign of Cancer on the eve of St. John the Baptist, the people assemble in the market places, or out in the open countryside to dance in the light of glowing bonfires.'

OLAUS MAGNUS, 1555.

Eve of St. John Baptist or Midsummer Eve	Dancing round Midsummer poles. Over the whole country.
Christmas and New Year. Winter	Lekstuga or indoor meetings for dancing. Now revived by folk dance societies.
Michaelmas, 29th September	Dance meetings in Northern Sweden, but generally obsolete.
All through the summer	At Skansen, the outdoor museum, Stockholm.

NOTE

The people of Sweden are extremely proud of the great variety and beauty of their regional costumes. Do not regard them as fancy dress. As they respect them, you are asked to respect them too.

The Editor

THE DANCES

TECHNICAL EDITOR, MURIEL WEBSTER
ASSISTED BY KATHLEEN P. TUCK

ABBREVIATIONS
USED IN DESCRIPTION OF STEPS AND DANCES

r—right ⎫ referring to   R—right ⎫ describing turns or
l—left ⎭ hand, foot etc.   L—left ⎭ ground pattern
C—clockwise   C-C—counter-clockwise

For descriptions of foot positions and explanations of any ballet terms the following books are suggested for reference:

A Primer of Classical Ballet (Cecchetti method). Cyril Beaumont.

First Steps (R.A.D.). Ruth French and Felix Demery.

The Ballet Lover's Pocket Book. Kay Ambrose.

REFERENCE BOOKS FOR DESCRIPTION OF FIGURES:

The Scottish Country Dance Society's Publications. Many volumes, from Thornhill, Cairnmuir Road, Edinburgh 12.

The English Folk Dance and Song Society's Publications. Cecil Sharp House, 2 Regent's Park Road, London N.W.1.

The Country Dance Book I–VI. Cecil J. Sharp. Novello & Co., London.

Plate 2
Floda, Dalecarlia

The body is held very upright in Swedish dancing, the men especially showing strength and vigour in their carriage. There is little movement of the body while steps are being performed except during a Waltz step, when there is a very slight swaying movement from side to side.

Unless otherwise described, the free hand or hands are held to the sides.

1. *Pair Dancing:* (A) as in Kadrilj. Both man and woman place r hands on partner's waist and l hands on partner's upper arm.

(B) as in Huppleken. The man places his r arm round partner's waist, his l arm is forward, elbow raised and l hand resting on partner's arm. The woman places her r hand on l arm of partner, her l elbow is bent and resting on partner's r arm. They stand facing each other, slightly sideways so that r shoulders are together if dancing C. When dancing C-C, l shoulders are together and the arms are reversed.

2. *Ring Dancing*, as in Huppleken. Men stretch out both arms and grasp side partner's upper arms; the women do the same. Dancers move round C.

To dance C-C, the men do 'arm clapping' as follows: they loosen their hold, swing arms upward and outward and grasp partners' arms again with a clapping movement. The leader indicates when this change should take place.

3. *Hand Clapping*, as in Huppleken. This is done without music after the Big Ring where partners are holding l hands. The woman places her open r hand over the clasped l hands; the man strikes it with his r hand, making a clapping sound. They release l hands and join each other's r hands; the man then swings his partner in front of him to get ready for Pair Dancing.

Walking and running steps are used extensively in all Swedish dancing. The man, and sometimes the women, stamp their feet (*Appell*) at the beginning or end of a musical phrase.

In Huppleken the above steps are used with less vigour and more elegance than in the other dances. When the men are hopping the women walk forward in a light and graceful manner, beginning with l foot. When running, the feet are not lifted from the ground as much as is usual in Swedish dancing, but are allowed to glide a little so that the dancing is graceful and elegant, as in a Waltz.

	Beats
East Gothland step (as in Renningen), 3/4 time.	
Step sideways on l foot.	1
Close r foot towards l foot.	2
Step forward on l foot.	and
Step forward on r foot.	3
Repeat, still beginning with l foot.	
Figuré step (as in Kadrilj), 2/4 time.	
Hop forward on l foot, placing r foot in front, toe touching the ground.	1
Hop forward on l foot, placing r foot beside l foot.	2
Repeat, hopping on r foot.	
Hopping step (as in Huppleken), 2/4 time.	
Jump forward on both feet.	1
Hop on l foot, lifting r knee high in front.	2
Jump forward on both feet.	1
Hop on r foot, lifting l knee high in front.	2
This constitutes two hopping steps. Repeat on alternate feet.	

Three-step (as in Huppleken), 3/4 time.
   Step forward on l foot.   I
   Close r foot behind l foot.   2
   Step forward on l foot.   3
   Repeat, beginning with r foot.

KADRILJ (*Quadrille*)

Region	Ovraby, Halland. Plates 3 and 4.
Character	With a certain dignity, as in most square dances.
Formation	Any even number of couples arranged in a square. The side dancers are called 1st couples, top and bottom dancers are called 2nd couples. See Diagram 1 (○ = woman, □ = man).

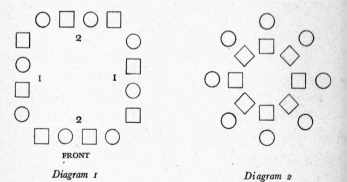

FRONT

Diagram 1   *Diagram 2*

22

Dance	MUSIC

1 THE BIG RING   A

All dancers turn outwards (pulling r shoulders back) and walk C for 8 bars of music, the men on the inside forming a back ring, the women on the outside (see Diagram 2).   1–8

All walk C-C in the same formation.   1–8

2 THE CHORUS (*Compliments, Figuré, Women Crossing, Arches*)

COMPLIMENTS   B

Partners hold inside hands at shoulder height, free hands to side.

1st couples walk forward towards each other, and bow or curtsey on 4th beat.   9–10

1st couples swing round without altering grasp and walk back to places.   11–12

2nd couples repeat.   13–16

FIGURÉ   C

Women hold skirts, men fold arms on chest.

1st couples dance 6 Figuré steps, lines advancing towards each other; each dancer then gives r hand to opposite partner, turns half to the R and falls back into opposite partner's place with 4 walking steps.   17–24

1st couples repeat to own places.   17–24

2nd couples repeat the above movement   17–24
across and back.   17–24

WOMEN CROSSING (LADIES' CHAIN)   D

1st women clap partners' hands on 1st beat, then cross to opposite woman's place giving r hands as they pass.   25–28

KADRILJ

From Ovraby. Noted by Erik Jenkler
Arranged by Arnold Foster

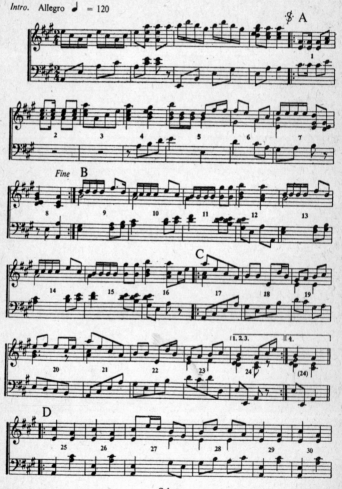

E

Play **A A, B, C C C C, D D, E E** *twice through. Finish* **A A.**

They then give l hands to the opposite men, who place r arms round their waists and swing them once round C.	
Repeat, crossing back to own place and swinging with own partners.	29–32
2nd women repeat the above movement across and back.	25–32

ARCHES   E

Couples are numbered as in Diagram 3.

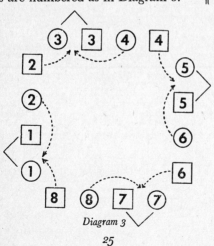

Diagram 3

The odd couples make arches:
8th man and 2nd woman go through 1st arch.
2nd man and 4th woman go through 3rd arch.
4th man and 6th woman go through 5th arch.
6th man and 8th woman go through 7th arch.

All dance with walking step.

Turn own partners as in Pair dancing.

Even couples make the arches and the movement is repeated by the odd couples.

33–38

39–40

33–40

3 WOMEN'S RING
Women join hands in an inner ring and walk C for 8 bars, while the men walk C-C and finish beside partners.

Partners link arms (women placing l arm in men's r arm) and all walk round C and finish in own place.

A
1–8

1–8

4 CHORUS as before.

9–40

5 THE GALLOP
The dance ends with a lively gallop, couples holding as in Pair dancing, and covering the following track:

The whole quadrille moves once round C-C, dancing the gallop steps without a turn at the sides, couples turning C across the top and bottom of the square.

A
1–8

RENNINGEN (*Weaving Dance*)

Region	Uppland. Plate 1.

Character	A dance-game symbolising the whole work of the loom: stretching the threads, winding, weaving, the movements of the shuttle, unwinding, and the hanging-up of the finished cloth.

Formation	A set of eight couples. The couples are numbered 1–8. Couples 1–6 join hands in a ring, couples 7 and 8 forming a cross inside the ring as described below and as shown in Diagram 1 (○ = woman, □ = man).

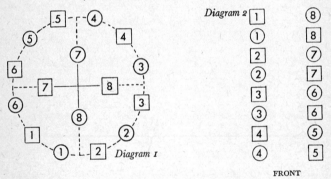

Diagram 2

Diagram 1

FRONT

7th and 8th men join r hands; 7th and 8th women do the same.

7th man holds the front wrist of 6th woman.

8th man holds the front wrist of 3rd woman.

7th woman holds the front wrist of 5th man.

8th woman holds the front wrist of 2nd man.

Three dancers stand between each arm of the cross.

Dance	MUSIC
	Bars

1 CROSS AND RING

    The dancers forming the ring walk with soft slow steps C while those forming the cross run or dance the East Gothland step C.

A
1–13

2a PROMENADE AND WINDING (running step)

    The ring is broken and 1st couple lead once round C, all others following as in a promenade.

    The men step in front of their partners and the 1st man leads the dancers into a maze, moving C.

B
14–29

2b UNWINDING (running step)

    All turn about; 8th woman now becomes the leader and leads the dancers two and a half times round C-C out of the maze and into two lines, as in Diagram 2 on page 27.

14–29

3a ADVANCE AND RETIRE, AND SHUTTLE

    Dancers join hands in two lines facing each other. All run 3 steps forward and stamp once (*Appell*).

    1st man gives his r hand to 8th woman, who gives him her l hand; they form the shuttle.

C
30–31

    Lines retire with 3 steps and 2 stamps, while the shuttle runs forward to the front between the two lines, turns round and stands still.

32–33

    Lines advance with 3 runs and 1 stamp.

34–35

Lines retire with 3 runs and 2 stamps, while the shuttle runs to the back, 1st man and 8th woman returning to own places. | 36–37

3b PAIR DANCING
    Couples hold as described under Arm Holds, 1A, and turn partners with running steps, or with 4 East Gothland steps, twice round C, to own places. | 38–41

3c ADVANCE AND RETIRE, AND SHUTTLE—as in 3a. | 42–49

3d PAIR DANCING—as in 3b. | 50–53

3e ADVANCE AND RETIRE
    Lines advance with 3 running steps and 1 stamp. | 54–57

    Lines retire with 3 running steps and 2 stamps.

    (There is no independent movement of the shuttle.)

4   RINGS | D
    Couples run C in a ring (twice round). | 58–65

    Couples swing round, still keeping women on R of men, and run C-C to finish in two lines facing one another (see Diagram 2). | 58–65

5 MARCH (walking step). Dancers sing the air during bars 72–76. | E

    Couples 1 and 8 join hands in a line of four and march to the front. The other couples face the back and march to the back, then | 66–76

Plate 3

RENNINGEN

From Uppland. Noted by Karl Gustavsson
Arranged by Arnold Foster

Play A, B B, C, D D, E.

turn to meet and also lead up in lines of 4
(see Diagram 3). At the front all cast off to
the R, the couples on 1st couple's side lead-
ing so that all progress C (see Diagram 4).
1st couple leads up the centre to finish in
a longwise set (couple 1 at front, couple 5
at back) as if showing the finished strip of
cloth.

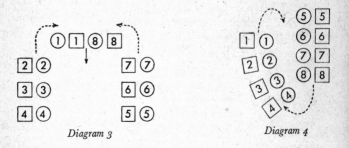

Diagram 3

Diagram 4

HUPPLEKEN (*Hopping Dance*)

ᵗᵉᶜₑₕᵗᵗᵗᵗᵗᵗᵗᵗₑₑₑₑ

Region	Found only at Floda, Dalecarlia. Plate 2.	
Character	An ancient form of wedding dance in which the 'Bridal Pair' is chosen and dressed in character, with the bridesmaids, best man and ushers also in bridal array. The dancing is dignified and elegant.	
Formation	Any number of couples face C. The men stand on the inside of the ring holding l hands with partners, free hands to sides.	

Dance	MUSIC
	Bars
1 BIG RING	A
All start with l foot and walk C. On the 3rd bar the men dance the Hopping step while the women continue to walk, smiling at their partners who hop higher and higher. This continues as long as the musician plays the A music.	1–12 with repeats
Short pause in the music while the dancers perform the Hand Clapping, as described under Arm Holds, No. 3.	
2 PAIR DANCING (see Arm Holds, No. 1B). The bridal couple begins and every second couple joins in. Dance C with running step.	B 13–20
Clap hands.	21

HUPPLEKEN

From Floda, Dalecarlia
Arranged by Arnold Foster

E *Dalecarlia Polska* ♩ = 144

Play A *(with repeats)*, B B B, C *(with repeats)*, D *(with repeats)*. E *(with repeats)*.

Dance C-C. During this time the other couples stand still and watch. 22–28

The watching couples repeat the same figure. 13–28

3 TO BUY THE FÖRDANS   B
One of the men leads his partner to the musician and gives him a coin to pay for his Fördans (preliminary dance). This couple then dances 'Pair Dancing', as in Figure 2, in front of the musician. 13–28

4 RING DANCING (see Arm Holds, No. 2)   C
All travel C. 29–44
Men perform Arm Clapping. 37
All travel C-C. 38–52

A quick, even running step is used throughout the figure.

5   THE CROOKED DANCE   D
    The man who has bought his Fördans leads   53–60
    his partner C, the other couples following. with
    His partner then leads the dancers in a   repeats
    chain (women in front of men), making any
    curved patterns that she pleases, as in a
    Farandole. Dancers finish in a ring.

6   DALECARLIA POLSKA   E
    All couples hold as in Pair Dancing and   61–72
    revolve continuously C. When a couple get with
    tired they may change to a Three-Step. To repeats
    do this, partners hold inside hands bent at
    shoulder level, free hands to sides.

These three dances and their tunes are taken (with the permission of
the author) from Gustaf Karlson's *Svenska folkdanser och sällskapsdanser*.
Huppleken was noted by Gustaf Karlson himself.

BIBLIOGRAPHY

BERGQUIST, N. W.—*Swedish Folk Dances*, 2nd ed. 1910, London. (Not always reliable as to source.)

KARLSON, G.—*Svenska folkdanser och sällskapsdanser.* 1944, published by Svenska Ungdomsringen för Bygdekultur, Stockholm. (Swedish folk dances and party dances.)

——*Samkväms- och gillesdanser.* 1941, Svenska Ungdomsringen, Stockholm. (Social and festive dances.)

LINDELÖF, E.—*Lekstugan.* 1913, Curwen, London. (Old Swedish dances, English edition.)

MALLANDER, I.—*Lärobok i folkvisedans.* 1935, Svenska Ungdomsringen, Stockholm. (How to dance folk dances.)

NILSSON, M. P.—*Våra danslekar.* 1915, Lund. (Dance-games.)

NORLIND, T.—'Svärdsdans och bågdans' in *Festskrift til H. F. Feilberg.* 1911, Copenhagen. (Sword dances and arch dances.)

——*Svensk folkmusik och folkdans.* 1930, Natur och Kultur, Stockholm. (Folk music and dances.)

REHNBERG, MATS.—*Swedish folk dances.* 1939, Stockholm. (No. 9 of the illustrated booklets issued by the Nordiska Museum and Skansen.)

RUNNQUIST-JAKOBSEN, G.—*Skånska danser.* 1927, Lund. (Dances of Scania, published by the magazine *Skånska folkminnen.*)

CEDERBLOM, G., & E. VON WALTERSTORFF.—*Svenska allmogedräkter.* 1921, Stockholm. (Swedish peasant dress.)

PRIMMER, K.—*Scandinavian peasant costume.* 1939, A. & C. Black, London. (Eight plates in colour and 64 pages of pencil drawings.)

SVENSSON, S.—*Folkdräkter.* 3 vols. (Booklets of the Nordiska Museum and Skansen. No. 4 covers South Sweden, No. 6 Central Sweden, and No. 8 Dalecarlia and the North.)

WISTRAND, P. G.—*Svenska folkdräkter.* 1907, Stockholm. (Swedish folk costume.)

THE FOLK LIFE FILMS of the Nordiska Museum, Stockholm.

RECORDS with folk-dance music are obtainable from Svenska Ungdomsringen för Bygdekultur, Hälsingegatan 4, Stockholm 6.